To Be A Man:

A Super Hero Manual Book

by

Daniel K. Arnold

Other Books

by Daniel K. Arnold:

The Super Hero Manual

Ever- Changing

Black Bird Ops

Journalists For Jesus

Obey God.

Culmination of a Miracle

Guest Speakers in Mental Health

This book is dedicated to the memory of Brian L. Arnold—a Father with so much love and protective purpose that he never once argued with my Mom in front of me. His legacy to Love and Protect lives on.

<u>To Be A Man:</u>

<u>A Super Hero Manual Book</u>

Chapter 1 – Introduction

Where does dignity come from? How can a man become secure in his manhood? What makes a man? What stretches us in the right way so that we can reach our potential?

Tell me, who am I? What is required of me to function? I want to live a meaningful life. Who can I talk to about male issues when most therapists are women?

God has answers and I am going to find them. He is not the author of confusion, but of peace—as to all the saints.

Sometimes we begin to find our dignity in our basic drives. Man wants completion. Man wants productivity. Man wants to spread His seed. We want our systems to work and to function like a young teenager.

As time passes by, and I begin to lose some faculties, I ask God to establish my new identity. We all pass through seasons. The initial puberty phase passes and we go through different stages of development.

What makes me a man? What makes you a man? Can this be stripped away from us or not? Age happens. Medications with diverse side effects happen. How do we keep our dignity?

In the Movie, "One Night With the King," a subject of King Xerxes was cut off from his physical masculinity along with all the men of Israel. How demoralizing is that? How can one go on like that? It would be extremely devastating.

My premise is a real man is someone who has found their purpose—to love and to protect. Dare to make a difference.

Modern medical practice many times has the side effect of the loss of sexual faculties.

This can spur on a midlife crisis. Or it can cause a man to search for what it means to really be a man… Maybe I can come to grips with this after all. How do you see me oh God? Past my drives? Past basic senses? Who am I to you?

I believe I can live with a passion so strong nothing can stop what God has begun in me!

I believe there's more to me than basic drives. I believe God has a purpose for me and for you! Lord, help us to find these blessings and dignity!

Who am I? Who are you? What matters in this life? Can I go on like a dried tree? A rejected eunuch?

Sometimes sanity comes at a price. This is me. This is my life.

Who am I God?

Is the corruption of God's simple drive pornography? How do we overcome this when we are tempted to test out a diminished drive? We need to give God our focus in everything! We need to be willing to lay down our lives in obedience to God. His plans are always better. We are in this world to love, honor and protect!

Daniel made a sacrifice to set
himself aside for God's work.
His life was not over after
becoming a eunuch. There was
hope and basic dignity left.

I write you today with hope and a
new mission. I wanted to
encourage the U.S. to encourage
adoption—to cut through the red
tape. It is time that I begin my
research project for the glory of
God.

<u>To Be A Man:</u>

<u>A Super Hero Manual Book:</u>

Chapter 2 - Pride Cometh Before
the Fall

I was big, I was bad, I was larger
than life. My sister said I had an
issue with pride, but I brushed
her away. With the support of
authorities at large I felt
unstoppable.

Then, I lost control. I became
captivated by a pressing horrific
issue in society and it burdened
me daily. I felt ready to impose
myself on everyone around me in

the name of this issue: Human Trafficking.

I stopped taking care of my health, my well-being, and reputation. I pushed forward with every bit of me until nothing was left.

I lost a great job at a preschool and found myself in a mental hospital involuntary.

As I pick up these pieces, I remember that God needs to be a priority in my life and I need to be His mouthpiece—no matter what I look like on paper.

Part of what helps me cope with sexual side effects, is the sheer passion of life—to live and be ready to pay a high price for what I believe in.

No longer do I impose venom on others about the issue of human trafficking-- now I look for a solution. At first, I thought a T-shirt needed to be made called "Adopt the Unwanted." Now that I know adoption costs tens of thousands of dollars in legal fees, I recommend what can be done now—providing foster care for scores of children!

The ability to spread my seed to create a child becomes a much smaller issue when I consider that there are unwanted children out there who want a family to call their own.

This is manhood—to love and protect society's most vulnerable. This is manhood, to unabashedly speak up for those who have no voice—not waiting for easy waters, but swimming upstream right now from a Crisis Unit.

I will not wait until things are ideal to make a difference; I will speak now!

Did you know that singles can be foster parents? Did you know that the government will help reimburse these parents for their expenses?

It is a big sacrifice to take care of a child who you do not have permanent custody over, but it is a must that someone steps up to the plate. Will that person be you?

Are you responsible enough to come to rescue of a beautiful little one? Contact a foster care service now!

Do your homework. See what it involves. Taking care of neglected, hurt children brings much purpose to life.

<u>To Be A Man:</u>

<u>A Super Hero Manual Book</u>

Chapter 3 - Today

Another day has passed and you or I may not be free. We may be in captivity in prison, a mental hospital, or feel like we are in our own mental prison. Guess what? God cares and so do I.

Begin to start associating with healthy people who are positive role models as far as it be possible. If you are fatherless, find a mentor. Do the best you can do and never give up.

Commit your life to helping
others over whining about your
own plight. You can make it
through. Begin to live your
bucket list now!

<u>To Be A Man:</u>

<u>A Super Hero Manual</u>

Chapter 4 - Turning The Table

If you are not quite stable for this responsibility, maybe a couple steps shy of losing control of yourself, remember you matter.

There is something you can do in this life that matters.

Maybe you can paint. Maybe you can compose music. Maybe you are good at cleaning. There's something out there that you love and can be used to benefit others.

Nothing should be able to hold you back from living a life of breakthrough!

Joni Erickson dived and became paralyzed from the neck down. Life did not seem worth living in her shoes, but she pressed on and began painting with her teeth.

Now a non-profit organization has been formed in her name.

She made an impact and there are more. Nelson Mandela made waves of change by writing from a prison in South Africa.

Nothing has to hold us back.

"But I'm alone. No one understands. I am a wreck and

do not even feel like a man anymore. All my joys are over."

I am telling you that your loss and turmoil can become your strength!

When a seed dies in the ground, it can grow up to form a large tree. We need to channel our difficulties into passionate power. We do have something to live for.

I spent a great deal of time battling with the thought that medicine was not allowing God to heal me. After awhile, the anguish in my brain became unbearable to face over the long haul. I decided to let go and get help!

I checked into Crisis Services at
CMHA-CEI and thought, I need
relief now. I cashed in my chips
and persuasive argument about
medicine noncompliance with
many people. No longer was I
the same poster-child. I was
aware immediately that I would
have to deal with sexual side
effects from this medication.

But then I recalled great leaders
in the Bible who had to face less
than ideal circumstances: Daniel
in the Lion's Den and Shadrach,
Meshach, and Abednego in the
Fiery Furnace who were all
under the care of the Prince of
the Eunuchs in Babylon. They
had to face the same plight as me,
but they did not stop living. They

lived monumental, purposeful
lives and became pivotal leaders
protecting their own people!

My life is not over. Your life is
not over due to circumstances.

<u>To Be A Man:</u>

<u>A Super Hero Manual</u>

Chapter 5 - Pressing On

Wherever you are, do not give up. Tell someone who cares what is tormenting you. Forgive others for anything that may have upset you. Realize that going on is possible. Do not take the bait! Avoid the drink of alcohol. Stop the dance with the devil. Whatever it is to you.

God cares about you right now in your pain. He will never leave you nor forsake you. Turn to God with all your worries. Surrender what you cannot control and just smile at life!

We must be thankful for what God has given us.

"Do not be anxious about anything, but in everything, by prayer and petition, with thanksgiving, present your requests to God and the peace of God that surpasses all understanding will guard your hearts and minds in Christ Jesus.

It is good to seek help from friends. If you are in Lansing, a great support system is either Justice in Mental Health Organization, employed by Certified Peer Support Specialists or Charter House employed by Community Mental Health workers. Get help and do

not make a drastic decision.
There are many resources you
can call in the case of an
emergency. Form a recovery
plan when you feel good—to call
those who can help in your time
of need.

<u>To Be A Man:</u>

<u>A Super Hero Manual</u>

Chapter 6- Super Heroes in God's Image

We may be Super Heroes, but we all have a weakness that keeps us humble as we are not God ourselves. Apostle Paul stated that "His power is made perfect in our weakness." We must keep consecrating ourselves to God and be in full reliance to Jesus as this life is temporary and not perfect.

Super Man had kryptonite and The Hulk had an anger issue as weaknesses. Oh God do help us. Sometimes I am somewhat like

Iron Man—so fast, so powerful, with enough pride to literally explode.

In past literature, I called myself Mr. Energy Plus on Lithium. Then, I upgraded to Black Bird Ops with Abilify. And now I am somewhere out on the stratosphere.

God can and will still pick up the pieces.

I wrote literature off my medication and now I am motivated despite any amount of medicine. I am a voice of change and awareness. I feel I can inspire others through literature. Some have already been touched

by what God has placed inside of
me.

The truth is I was birthed for a
purpose, greater than the mind
can conceive—for my being
makes up the Lord's divine
handiwork.

<u>To Be A Man:</u>

<u>A Super Hero Manual</u>

Chapter 7 - Allies and Opponents

As we go through seasons as people, it important to realize that not everyone is going to support our journey to take a stand to love and protect.

Some will seem to hate us for simply being us. This can be discouraging, but the Bible says we will be persecuted.

I need to grow in the area of responding to anger. "A gentle answer turns away wrath."

As men, it may feel whoever is dominant and strongest in

physical battle is the most
masculine. However,
self-control, is what preserves us
and our circle.

Would we hold our tongue to
protect those around us? Would
we remain silent to let an issue
die down in humility?

There are times to be quiet.
There are times to speak out. Be
prayerful about how you respond
to your enemies and may I do the
same.

The best response would seem to
be to leave the moment—with
prayer and careful consideration.
If we do not know something
wise to say, let's not say
anything at all!

To Be A Man:

A Super Hero Manual Book

Chapter 8 - Strength for Today

"Do not worry about tomorrow; for tomorrow will take care of itself. There are enough worries in today."

Take things slow. Peacefully. When Super Heroes are in recovery, they may have to disappear off the map for awhile. "Self care" is a must. This I did not learn until I crashed and burned.

Today, I am slowly learning to take on challenges again-- One piece at a time. "Rome was not built in a day."

What does God want me to do
today? I heard a wonderful quote
before, "Preparation is ministry."
Let us move forward with our
friends and family forward now.

To Be A Man:

A Super Hero Manual Book

Chapter 9 - Kryptonite

How does someone such as myself stay away turning into my enemy of myself—David Spinx? Pride does come before the fall, after all.

Consistent investment is much better than scatter shot for my personality. Consistent investment involves greater accountability.

Today, I went to my church again and people were happy to see me. I feel a little weak from all of my heavy involvement leading to sickness, but this is a

new day-- friends and family
miss me!

Invest on passions instead of
pleasure. Pleasure is passing, but
what we are passionate about, we
tend to be more committed to, no
matter how the world sees it!

When of the greatest modern
films, "The Passion of the Christ"
graphically depicts a conception
of the torture Jesus faced for us
on the cross. His closest friends
did not understand Him until His
death, but He still changed the
world.

I want to be a world-changer and
the Lord is not done with me yet!
There is hope and a future for us!

<u>To Be A Man:</u>

<u>A Super Hero Manual Book</u>

Chapter 10 – Moving Forward

Keep plugging away. Do what you love. Interact with the people who care about you. Do not ever give up.

Life comes in seasons and the storm will pass. In the midst, do what you adore in small doses—daily expanding the threshold without being overwhelmed.

One day I will work again and so will you. But for today, we must invest in people, volunteering and being the great people we were made to be. Walk away from situations that demand more than you can handle. You know your threshold and so does God. Plug away where you can make a dent!

I am very excited to be alive and sharing with you. I am happy that my head is no longer spinning and I feel like I am in the right place at the right time.

This book thus far has been sown in tears, pains, and the need for breakthrough. I am discovering this breakthrough as I write this book and I hope that you are too!

You can be the voice to bring hope and inspiration wherever you are. I recall nursing staff at my last mental hospital visit encouraging me in my faith.

They took the time to validate and listen to my perspective. I believe I was able to bring something to the table despite my lack of freedom at the time.

A true man never gives up. He lives this life with meaning and purpose no matter what the world throws at him.

Sometimes I get confused about how to live my life. There are many voices out there: The voice of family, the voice of change, the voice of rebellion, and the voice of those who always seem to agree with us.

Not every voice can be right at the same time. As men, we must draw our line in the sand and stand for what we believe in despite mountains of pressure.

This is not the hardest part of the war for me. The hardest part is switching gears to back down from a position that may have been a drastic mistake.

I spent 120 days standing against psychotropic medicine in my war for recovery. It seemed like the spiritual thing to do. But when my head spinned to the point of towel. I tapped out and chose to take psychotropic medicine. The war ended right there.

Before I was worried my passions would go out the window during this process, but hear I write you with the loss of some of my faculties and the gaining of others. I drew my line in the sand and then I crossed it for the whole professional world to see.

I've lost my job. I've lost important meetings with professionals. I've lost my physical manhood chemically.

Somehow, people stand by me still and never have disappeared. My family is here for me. My church body has missed me.

We are in this together. When life doesn't seem right, we who have tackled some of the storm can help someone who may be a different point in the journey.

When we help one another, it helps answer the question of the purpose of us enduring the pain.

Jesus went through every pain known to man so that He could relate to us. He is interceding for us even now.

Philippians 2:1-4

"If there be therefore any consolation in Christ, if any comfort of love, if any fellowship of the Spirit, if any bowels and mercies,

 Fulfil ye my joy, that ye be likeminded, having the same love, being of one accord, of one mind.

 Let nothing be done through strife or vainglory; but in lowliness of mind let each esteem other better than themselves.

Look not every man on his own things, but every man also on the things of others."

To Be A Man:

A Super Hero Manual Book

Chapter 11 - Conclusion

What can we take away from this short book? Our lives matter to each other and to God. We are significant human beings with a purpose.

Do not ever stop dreaming about the possibilities of tomorrow! "All things are possible with God."

There are many good quotes out there to inspire us and good people to fellowship with if we look in the right circles.

Sometimes it feels like all our bridges are burned but that's only a façade.

The truth is you and I were made for a reason. And just because we do not hold a prestigious title any longer, does not mean we can't help change the world!

All of our past experiences become part of our recovery story to impact others.

Make a difference today by giving thanks for what we do have and listening to others who may be going through even worse.

"Count your blessings one by one" and make an impact. Find your sphere of influence and invest, invest. Never give up.

Never back down. Let the Lord
lead you!

9 781986 027410